SELECTIONS FROM
O BROTHER WHERE ART THOU?

Artwork and photos courtesy of Touchstone Pictures

ISBN 0-634-06447-9

HAL•LEONARD®
CORPORATION

7777 W. BLUEMOUND RD. P.O. BOX 13819 MILWAUKEE, WI 53213

For all works contained herein:
Unauthorized copying, arranging, adapting, recording or public performance is an infringement of copyright.
Infringers are liable under the law.

Visit Hal Leonard Online at
www.halleonard.com

CONTENTS

THE BIG ROCK CANDY MOUNTAIN

Words, Music and Arrangement by
HARRY K. McCLINTOCK

Moderately

One

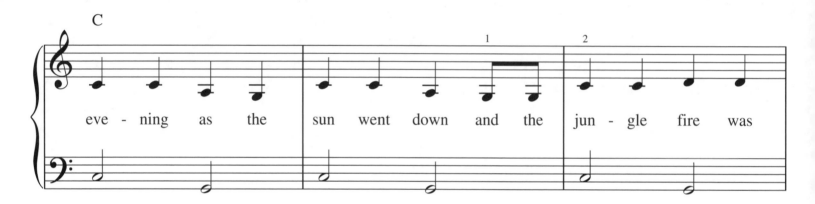

eve - ning as the sun went down and the jun - gle fire was

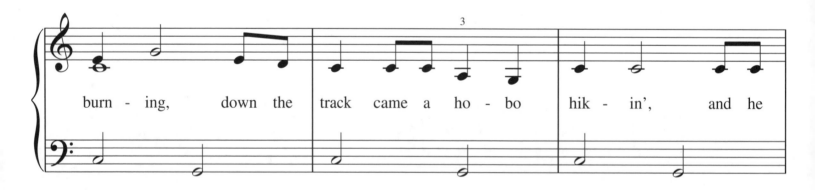

burn - ing, down the track came a ho - bo hik - in', and he

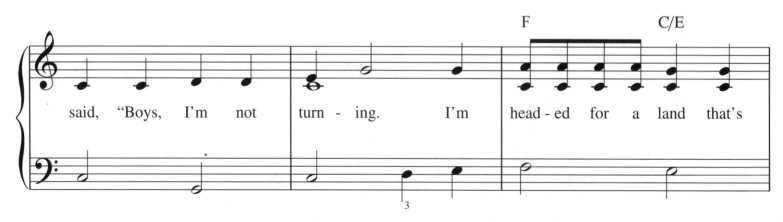

said, "Boys, I'm not turn - ing. I'm head - ed for a land that's

Copyright © 1955 by The Estate of Harry McClintock
Copyright Renewed
All Rights Reserved   Used by Permission

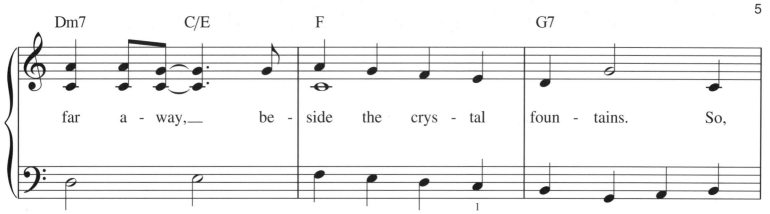

far a - way,__ be - side the crys - tal foun - tains. So,

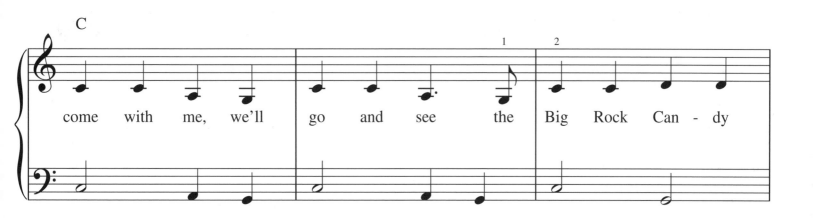

come with me, we'll go and see the Big Rock Can - dy

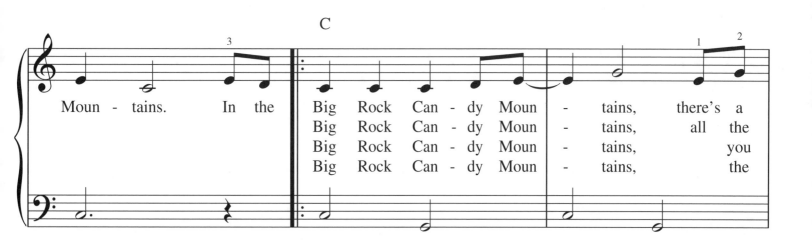

Moun - tains. In the | Big Rock Can - dy Moun - tains, there's a
Big Rock Can - dy Moun - tains, all the
Big Rock Can - dy Moun - tains, you
Big Rock Can - dy Moun - tains, the

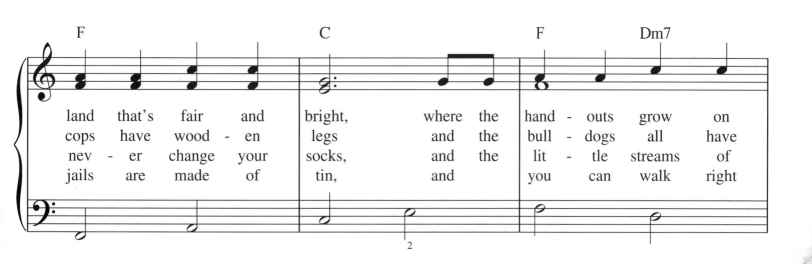

land that's fair and | bright, where the | hand - outs grow on
cops have wood - en | legs and the | bull - dogs all have
nev - er change your | socks, and the | lit - tle streams of
jails are made of | tin, and | you can walk right

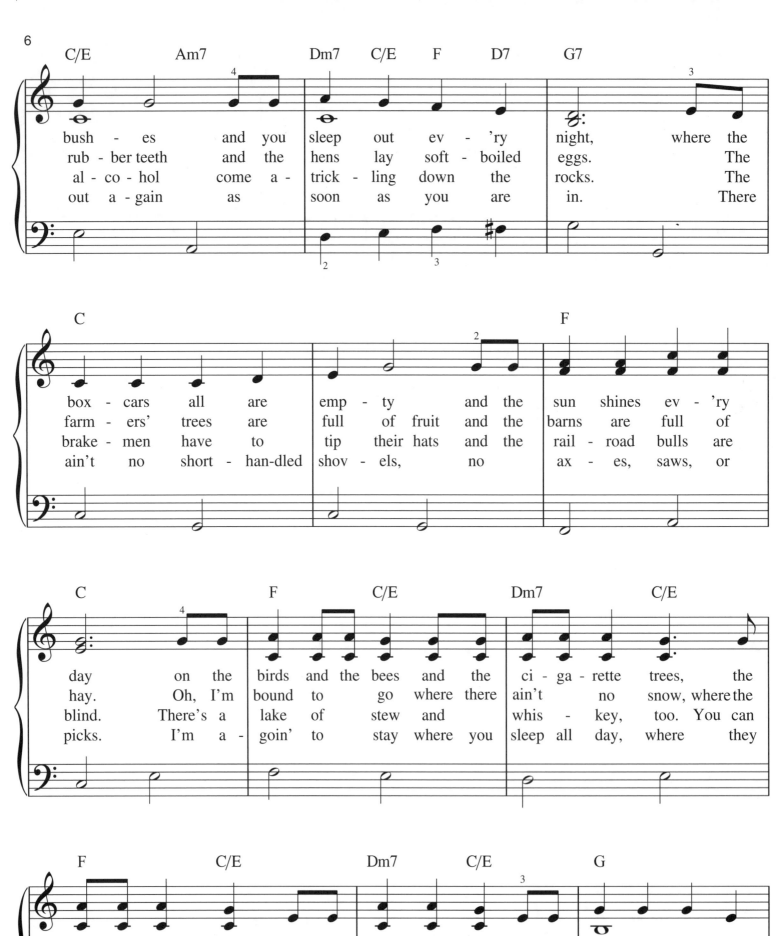

Moun - tains. In the Moun - tains.
Moun - tains. In the Moun - tains.
Moun - tains. In the *(Instrumental)*

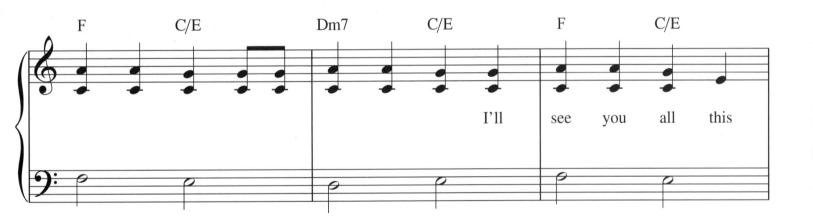

I'll see you all this

com - in' fall___ in the Big Rock Can - dy Moun - tains.

YOU ARE MY SUNSHINE

Words and Music by JIMMIE DAVIS
and CHARLES MITCHELL

Copyright © 1930 by Peer International Corporation
Copyright Renewed
International Copyright Secured   All Rights Reserved

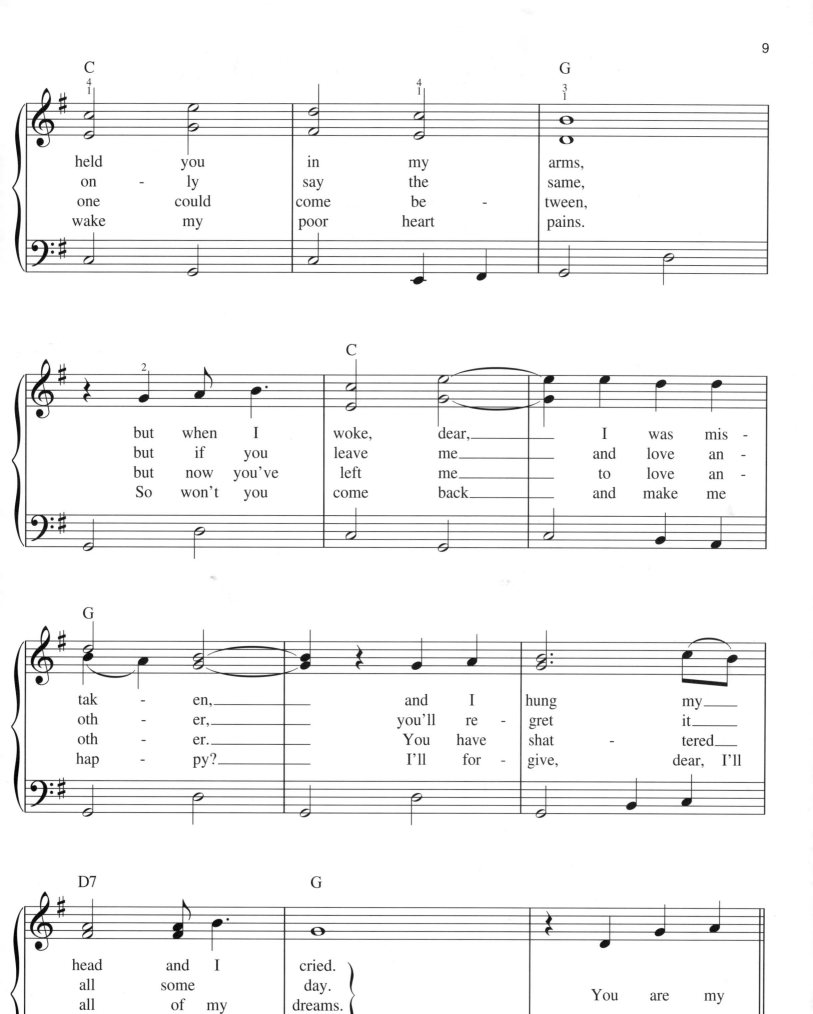

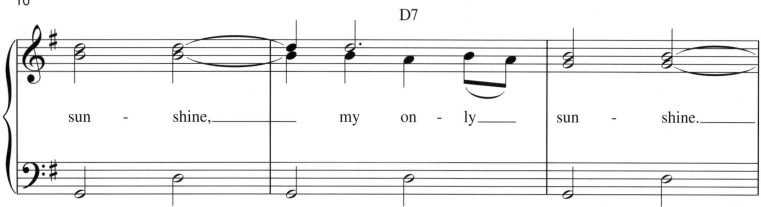

sun - shine,_____ my on - ly_____ sun - shine._____

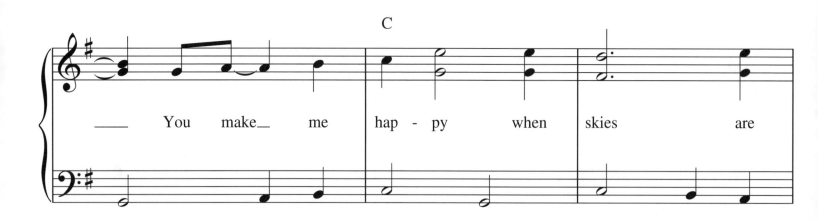

_____ You make__ me hap - py when skies are

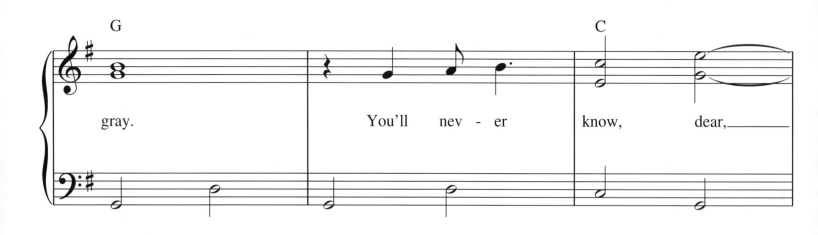

gray. You'll nev - er know, dear,_____

_____ how much I love_____ you._____ Please don't

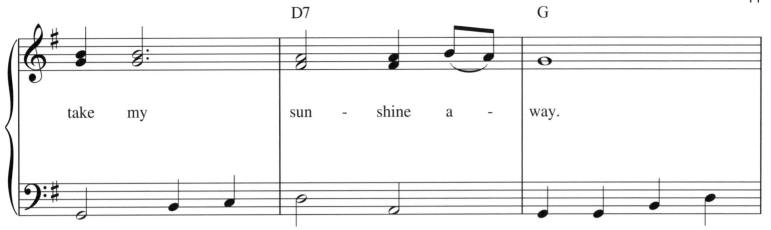

take my sun - shine a - way.

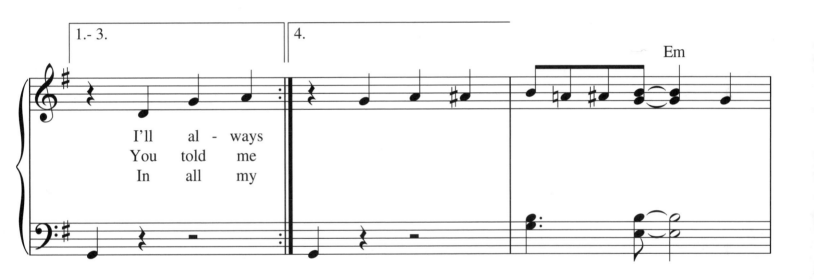

1.- 3.

4.

Em

I'll al - ways
You told me
In all my

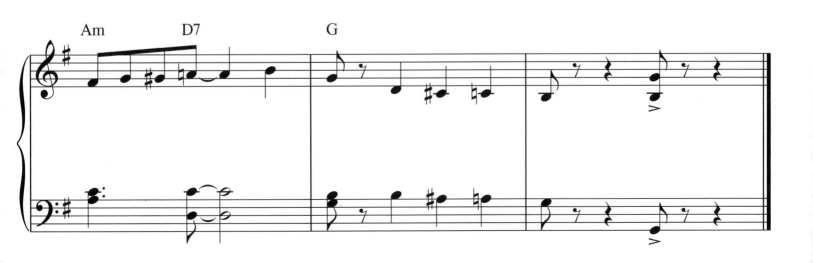

Am   D7   G

DOWN TO THE RIVER TO PRAY

Traditional

Moderately, in one

With pedal

Copyright © 2003 by HAL LEONARD CORPORATION
International Copyright Secured   All Rights Reserved

Oh, sis - ters, let's go down, let's go

Oh, broth - ers, let's go down, come on

let's go down, come on down. don't you

come on down, wan - na go down? down.

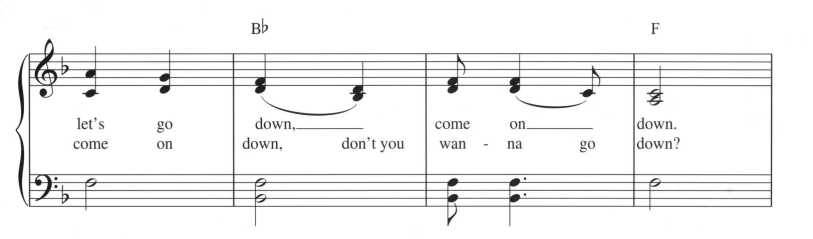

Oh, sis - ters, let's go down, down in the

Oh, broth - ers, let's go down, down in the

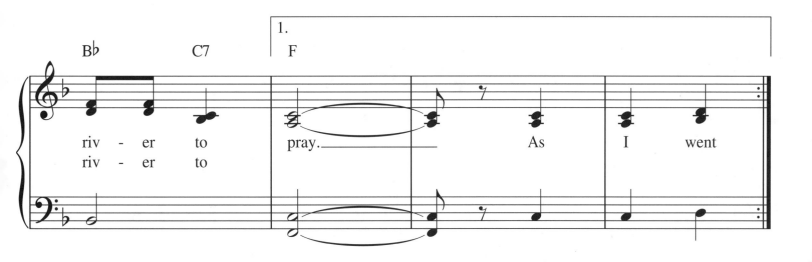

1.

riv - er to pray. As I went

riv - er to

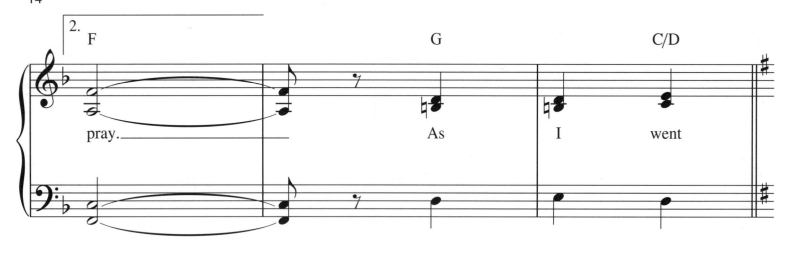

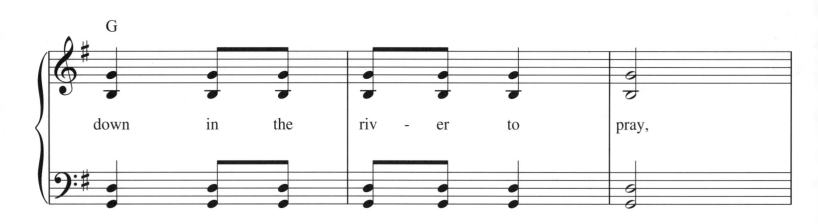

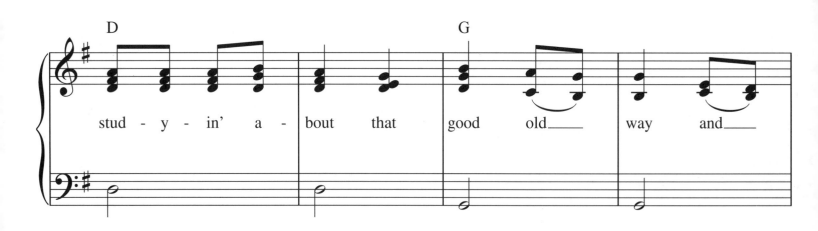

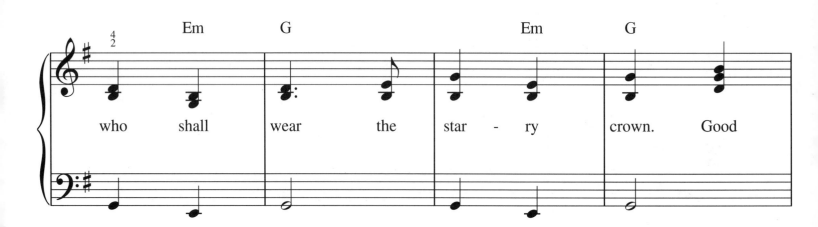

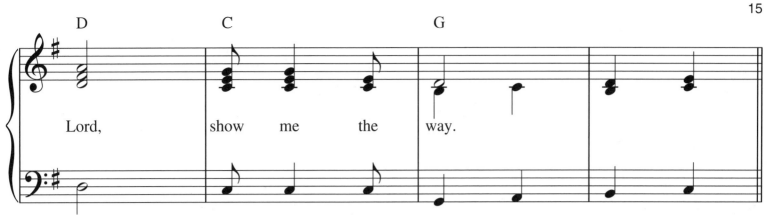

Lord, show me the way.

Oh, fa - thers let's go down,____

let's go down,____ come on____ down.

Oh, fa - thers, let's go down,____

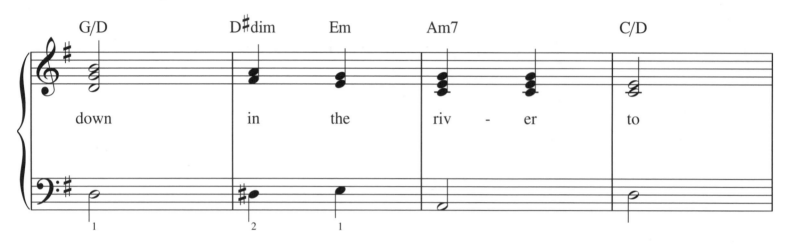

More broadly

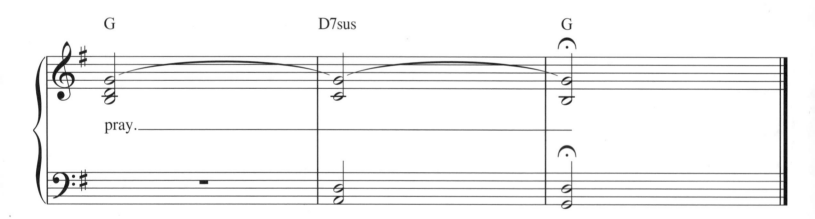

Additional Lyrics (if needed)

3. Oh, mothers, let's go down,
   Let's go down, come on down.
   Oh, mothers, let's go down,
   Down in the river to pray.

4. Oh, sinners, let's go down,
   Let's go down, come on down.
   Oh, sinners, let's go down,
   Down in the river to pray.

I AM A MAN OF CONSTANT SORROW

Words and Music by
CARTER STANLEY

Moderately fast Country

Copyright © 1953 by Peer International Corporation
Copyright Renewed
International Copyright Secured   All Rights Reserved

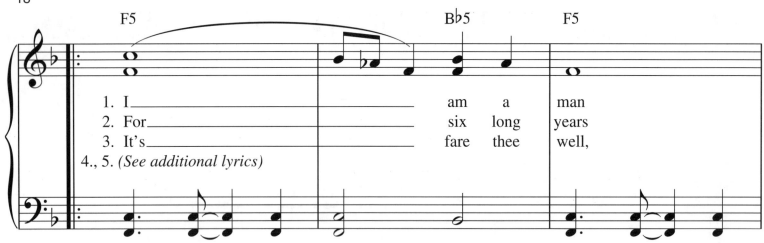

1. I_____ am a man
2. For_____ six long years
3. It's_____ fare thee well,
4., 5. *(See additional lyrics)*

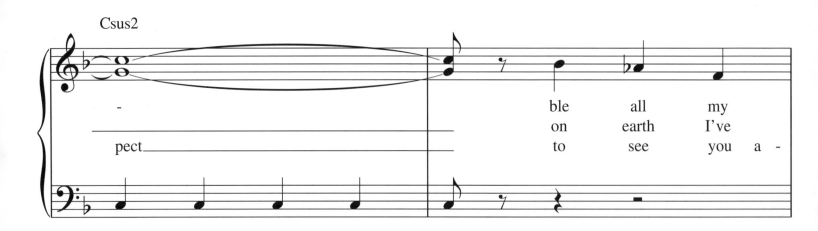

of   con - stant   sor - row._____   I've   seen   trou -
I've   been   in   trou - ble,_____   no plea - sure   here
my   own   true   lov - er,_____   I   nev - er   ex -

_____   ble   all   my
_____   on   earth   I've
pect_____   to   see   you   a -

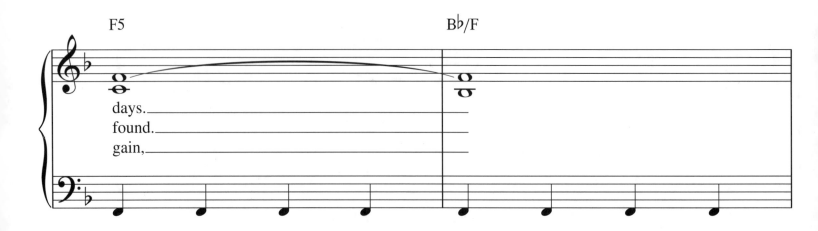

days._____
found._____
gain,_____

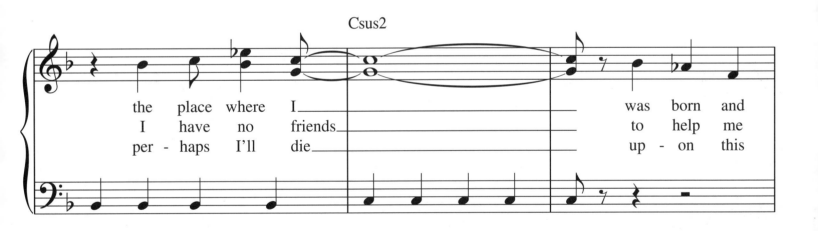

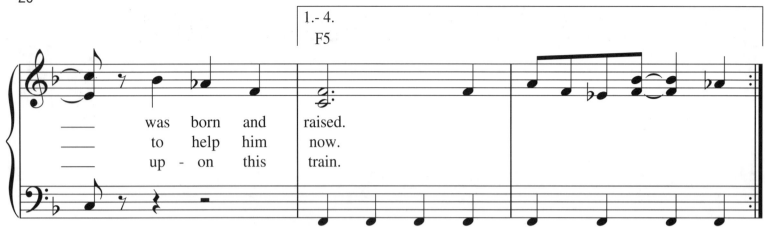

was   born   and   raised.
to   help   him   now.
up - on   this   train.

shore.

Additional Lyrics

4. You can bury me in some deep valley
   For many years where I may lay,
   And you may learn to love another
   While I am sleeping in my grave.
   While he is sleeping in his grave.

5. Maybe your friends think I'm just a stranger;
   My face you never will see no more.
   But there is one promise that is given:
   I'll meet you on God's golden shore.
   He'll meet you on God's golden shore.

KEEP ON THE SUNNY SIDE

Words and Music by
A.P. CARTER

Copyright © 1928 by Peer International Corporation
Copyright Renewed
International Copyright Secured   All Rights Reserved

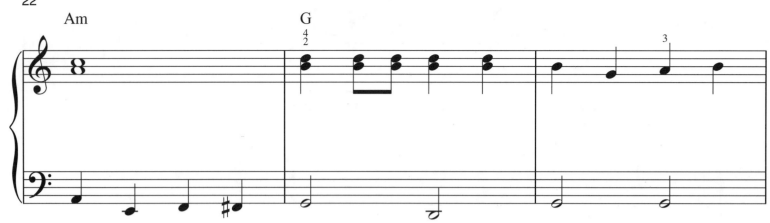

There's a dark and a
Though the storm and its
Let us greet with a

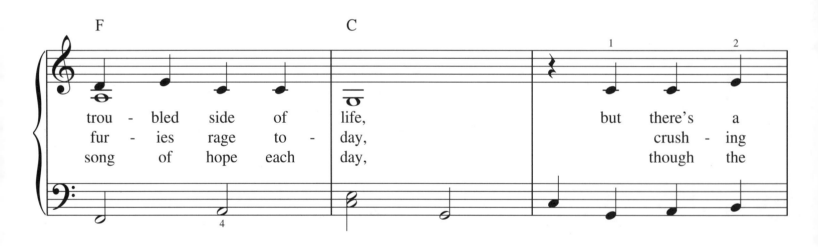

trou — bled side of life, but there's a
fur — ies rage to — day, crush — ing
song of hope each day, though the

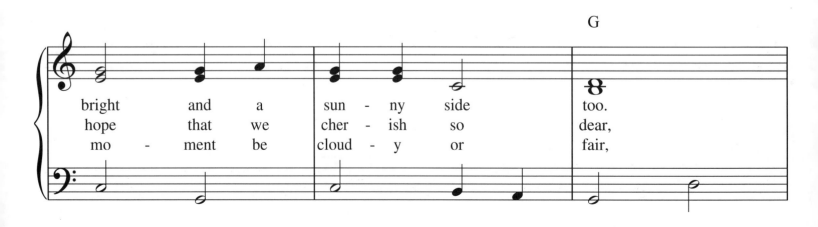

bright and a sun — ny side too.
hope that we cher — ish so dear,
mo — ment be cloud — y or fair,

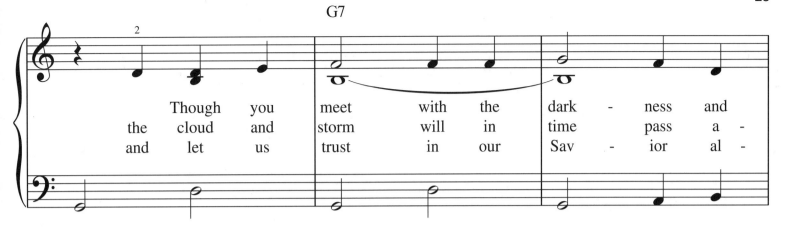

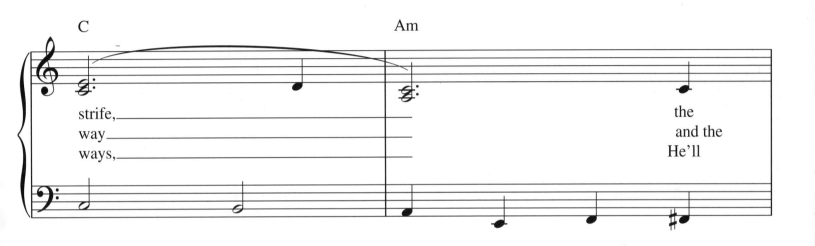

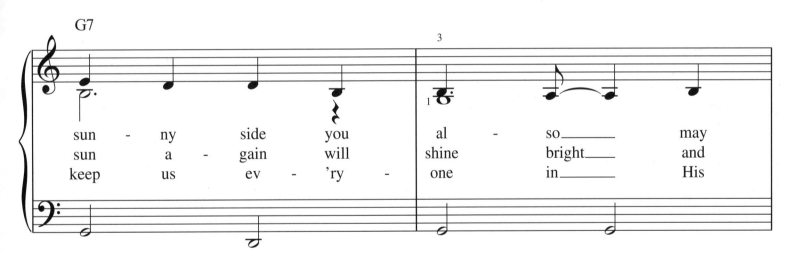

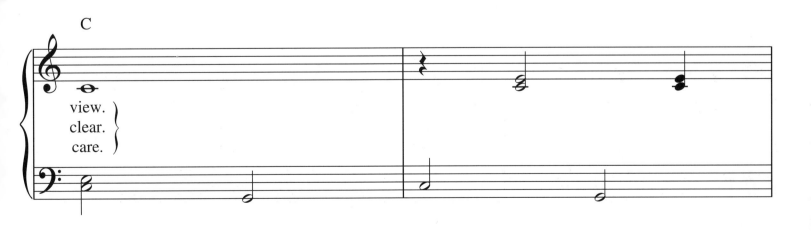

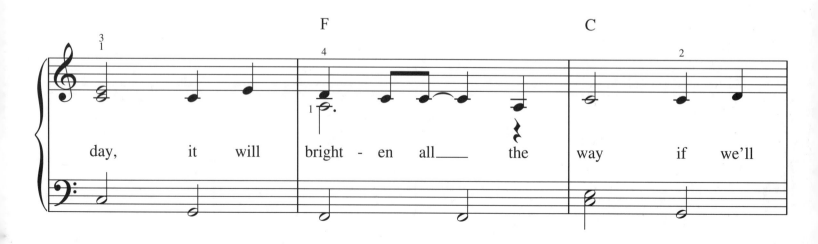

I'LL FLY AWAY

Words and Music by
ALBERT E. BRUMLEY

© Copyright 1932 in "Wonderful Message" by Hartford Music Co.
Renewed 1960 Albert E. Brumley & Sons (SESAC)/admin. by ICG
All Rights Reserved   Used by Permission

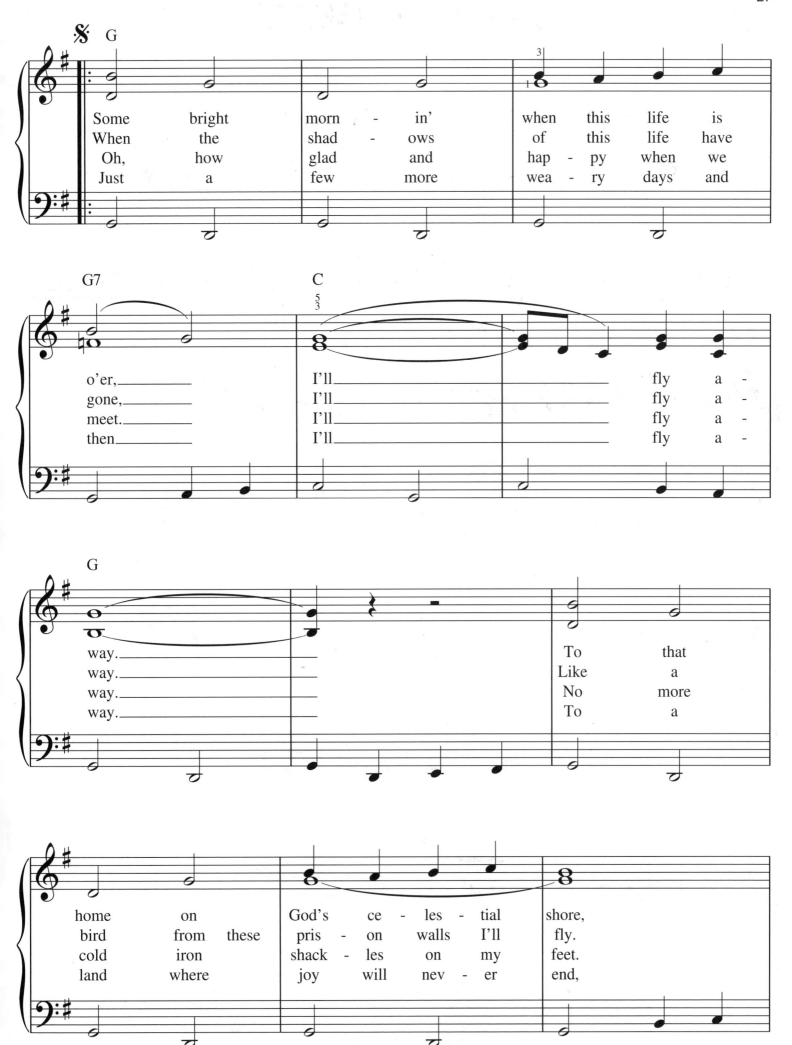

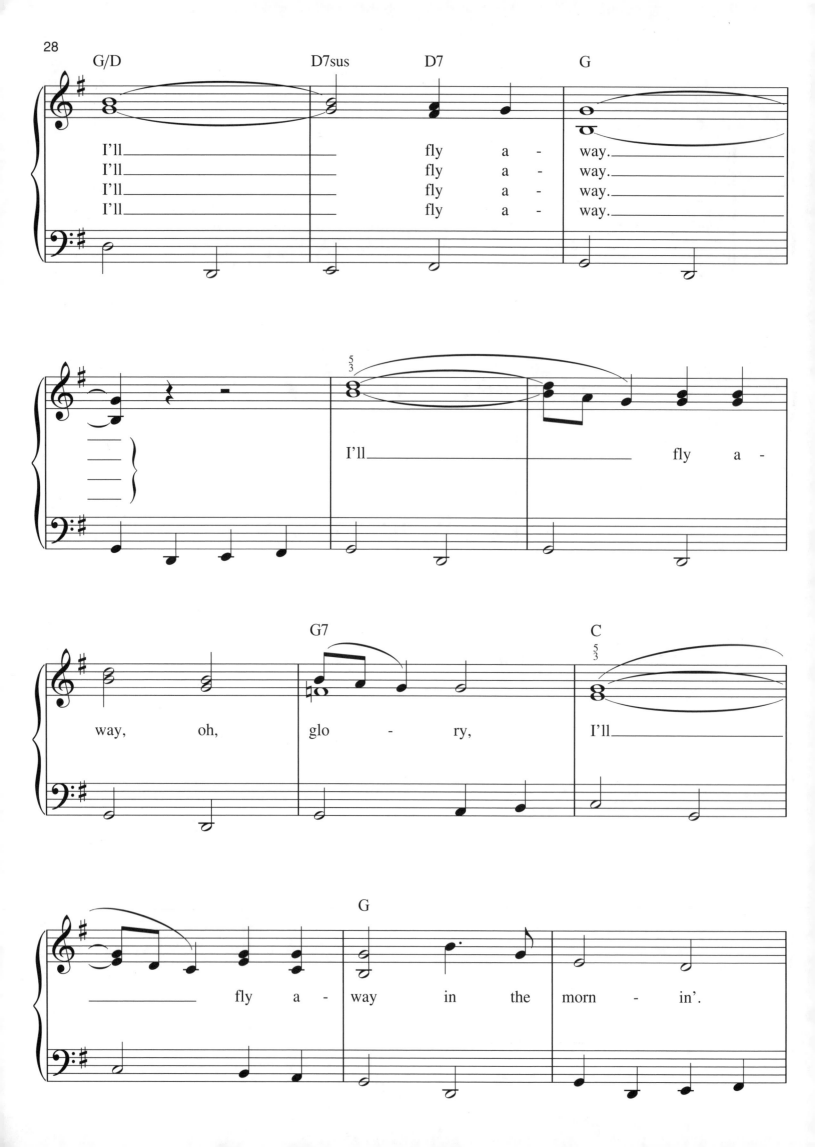

When I die, hal - le - lu - jah by____ and

To Coda ⊕

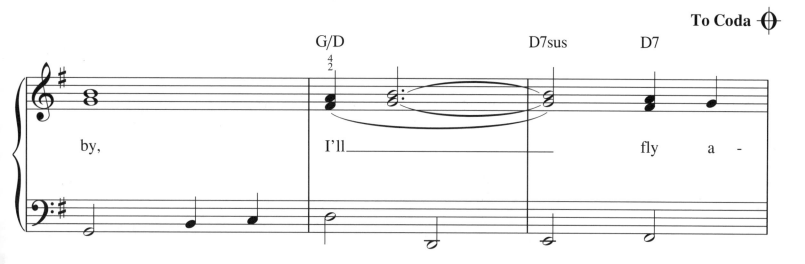

G/D   D7sus   D7

by,   I'll____   fly a -

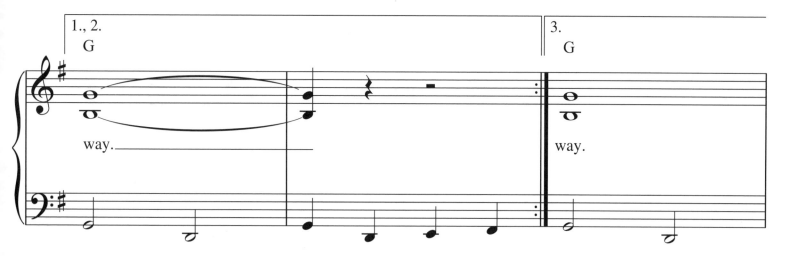

1., 2.
G

3.
G

way.____   way.

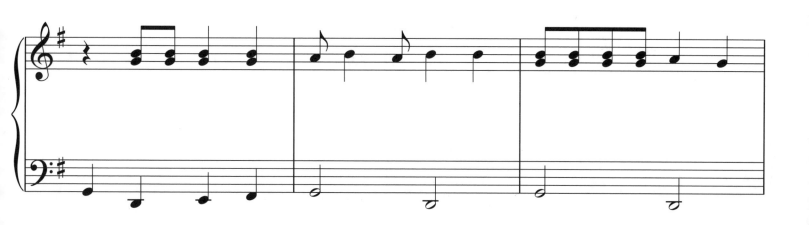

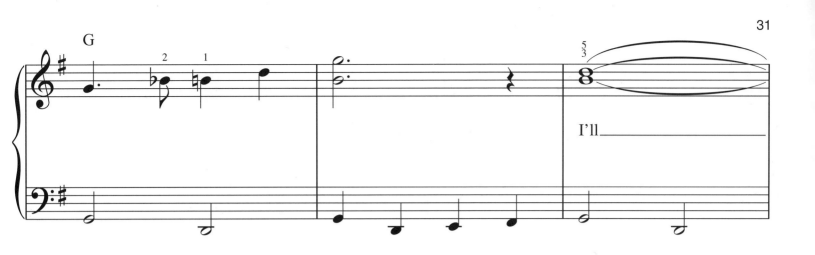

I'll _____ fly a - way, oh, glo - ry,

I'll _____ fly a - way in the

morn - in'. When I die, hal - le - lu -

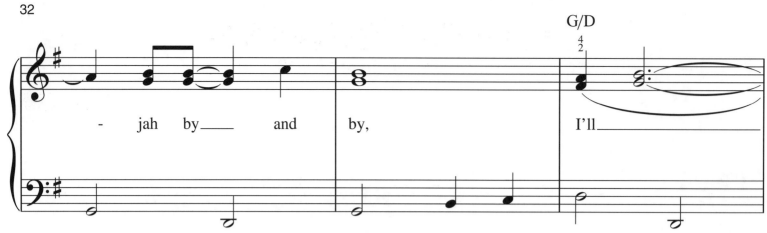

-jah by___ and by, I'll___

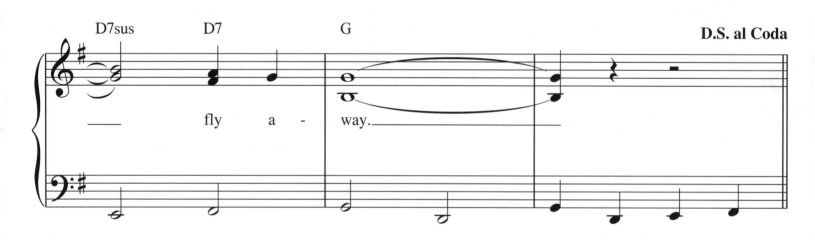

D7sus   D7   G   **D.S. al Coda**

___ fly a - way.___

CODA

G   G/D

way.___   I'll___

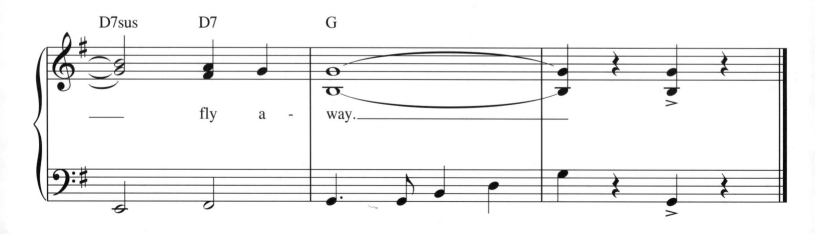

D7sus   D7   G

___ fly a - way.___

IN THE HIGHWAYS
(I'll Be Somewhere Working for My Lord)

Words and Music by
MAYBELLE CARTER

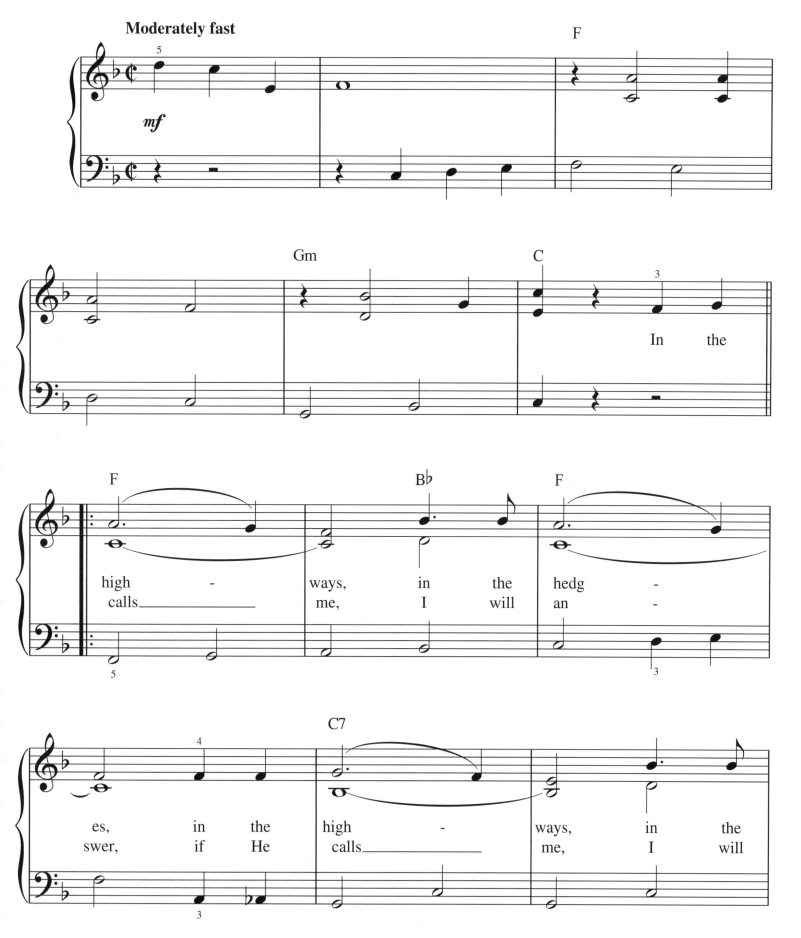

Copyright © 1965 by Peer International Corporation
Copyright Renewed
International Copyright Secured   All Rights Reserved

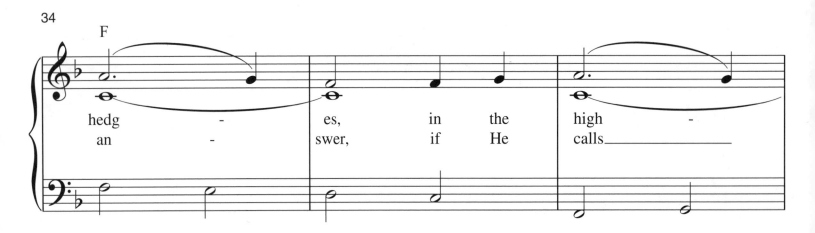

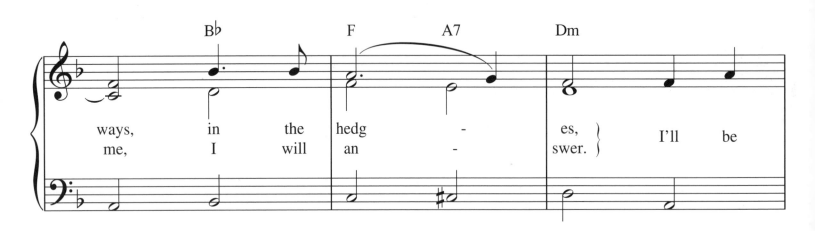

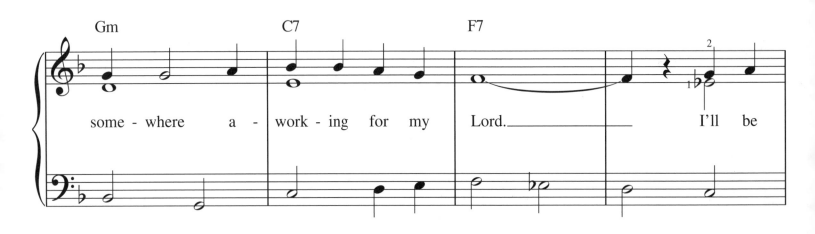

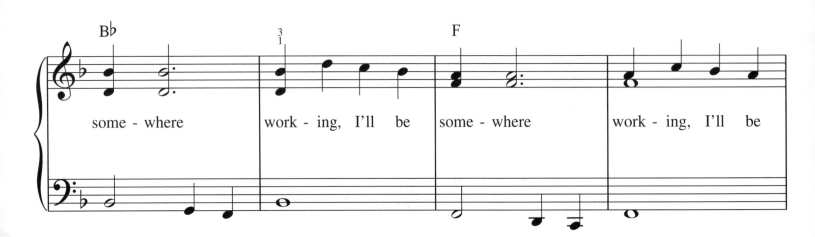

some - where a - work - ing for my Lord.____

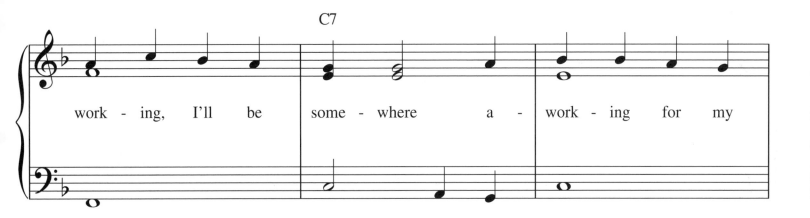

____ I'll be some - where work - ing, I'll be some - where

work - ing, I'll be some - where a - work - ing for my

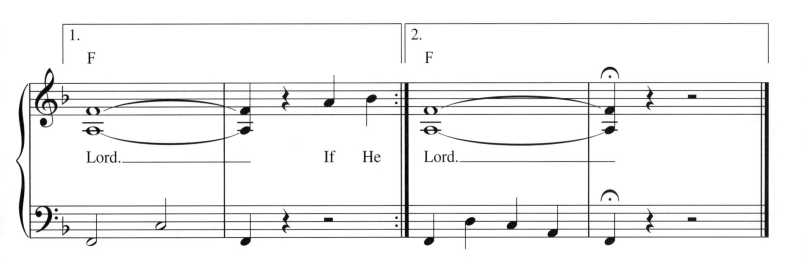

Lord.____ If He Lord.____

I AM WEARY
(Let Me Rest)

Words and Music by
PETE (ROBERTS) KUYKENDALL

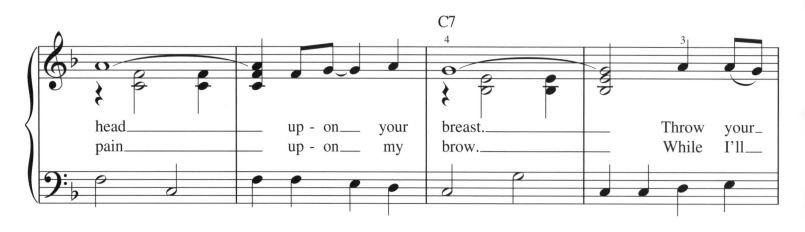

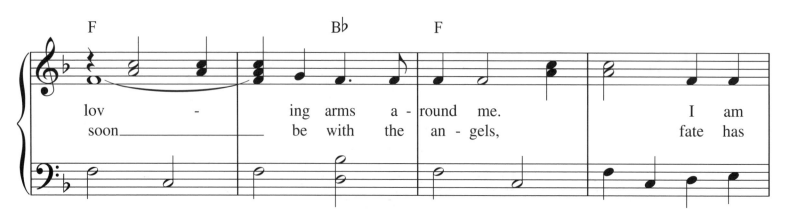

Copyright © 1964 (Renewed 1997) Wynwood Music Co., Inc.
All Rights Reserved   Used by Permission

To Coda

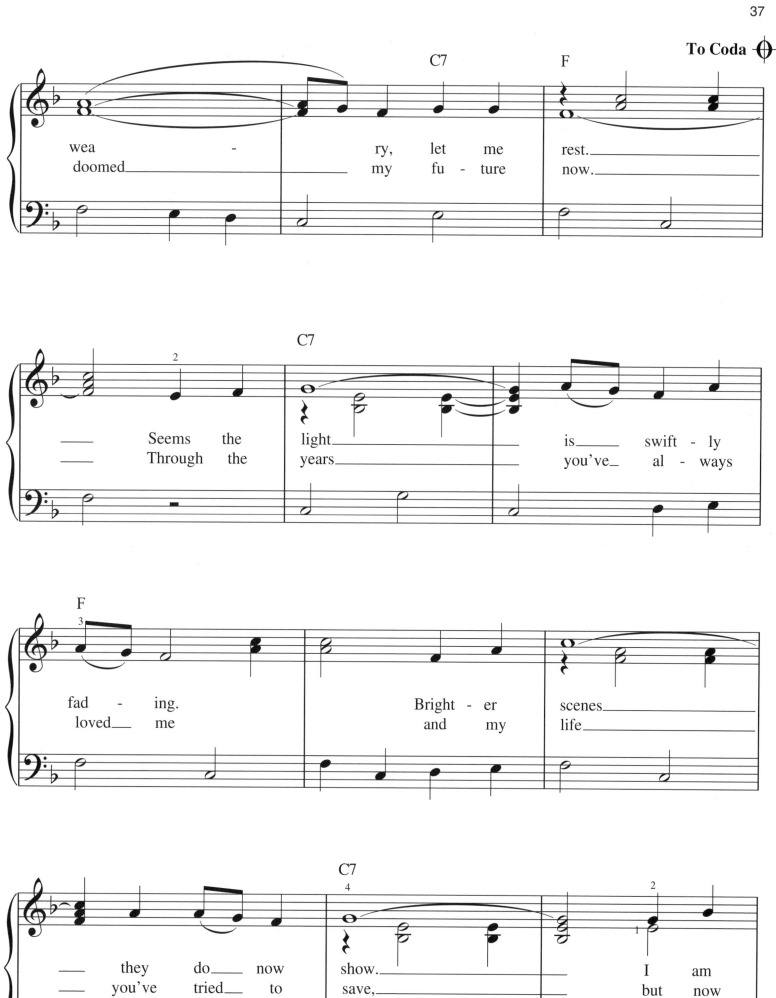

IN THE JAILHOUSE NOW

Words and Music by
JIMMIE RODGERS

Copyright © 1928 by Peer International Corporation
Copyright Renewed
International Copyright Secured   All Rights Reserved

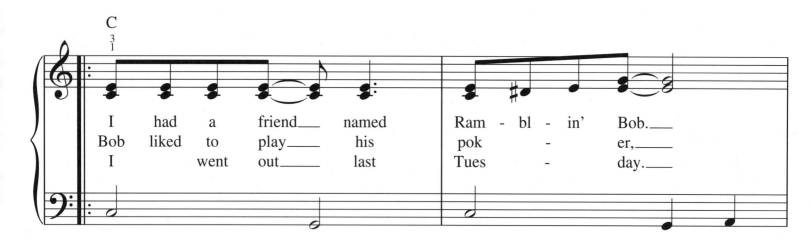

I had a friend___ named Ram - bl - in' Bob.___
Bob liked to play___ his pok - er,___
I went out___ last Tues - day.___

He used to steal,___ gam - ble and rob.___ He
pi - noch - le with Stan Yo - ker,___ but
I met a girl named Su - sie.___ I

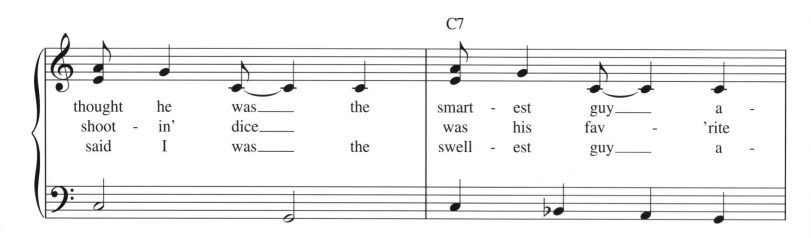

thought he was___ the smart - est guy___ a -
shoot - in' dice___ the was his fav - 'rite
said I was___ the swell - est guy___ a -

round.
game. But
round. Well, Well, we

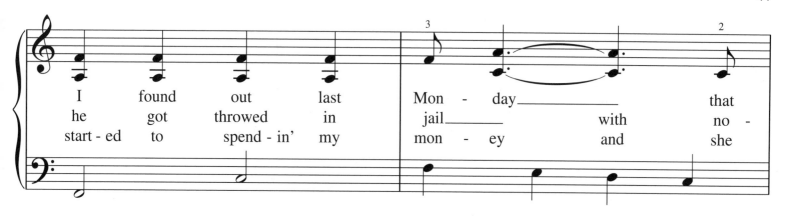

I found out last Mon - day_____ that
he got throwed in jail_____ with no -
start - ed to spend - in' my mon - ey and she

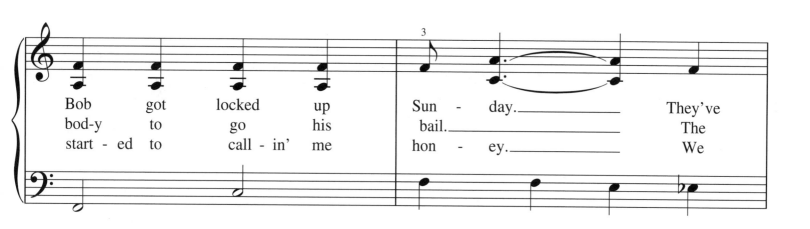

Bob got locked up Sun - day._____ They've
bod - y to go his bail._____ The
start - ed to call - in' me hon - ey._____ We

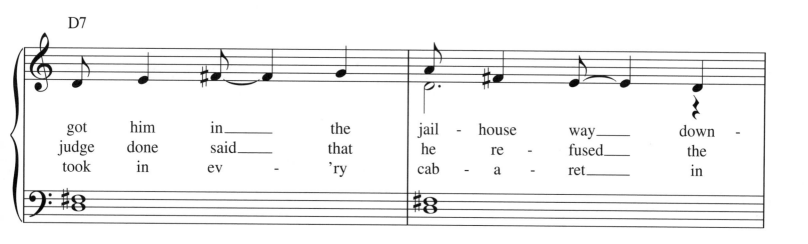

D7

got him in_____ the jail - house way_____ down -
judge done said_____ that he re - fused_____ the
took in ev - 'ry cab - a - ret_____ in

G7   **N.C.**

town.   He's in the jail - house
fine.   He's in the jail - house
town.   We're in the jail - house

42

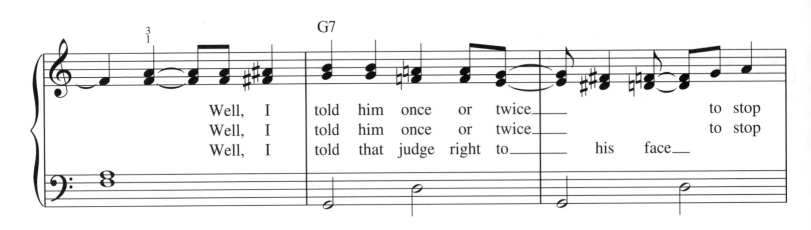

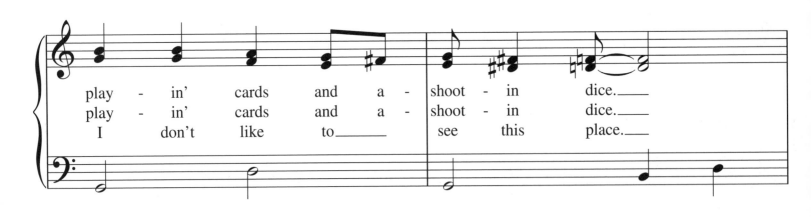

ANGEL BAND

Words and Music by
RALPH STANLEY

Copyright © 1958, 1978 by Fort Knox Music Inc. and Trio Music Company, Inc.
Copyright Renewed
International Copyright Secured   All Rights Reserved
Used by Permission

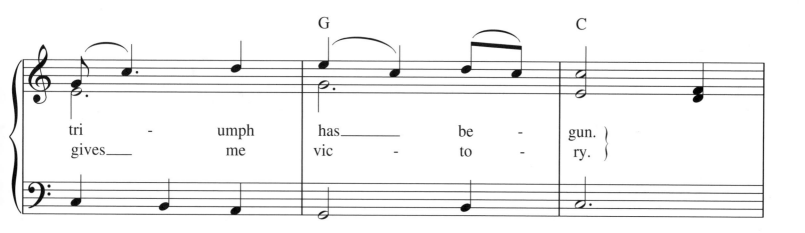

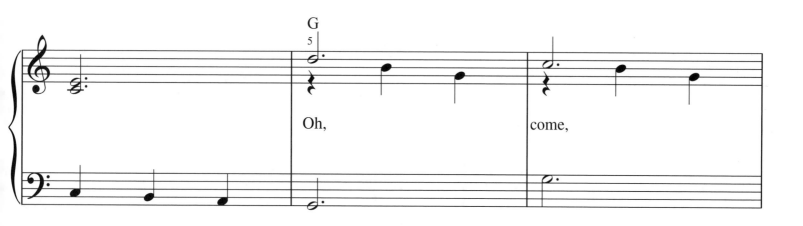

an - gel band._____ Come

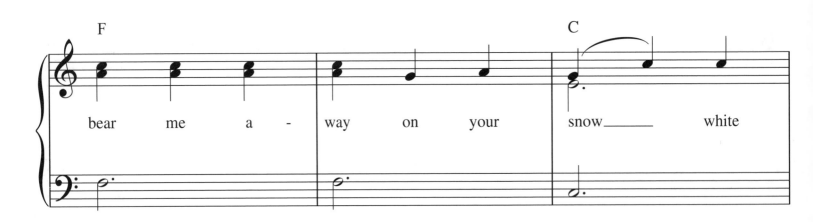

and a - round_____ me_____ stand. Oh,

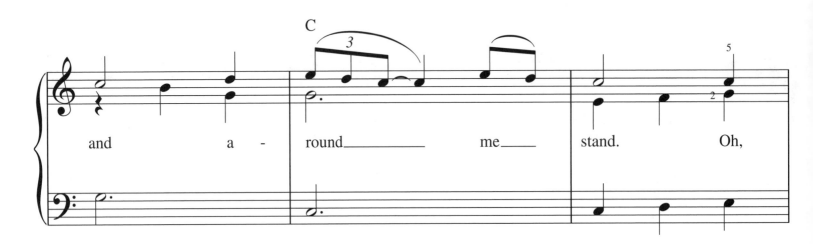

bear me a - way on your snow_____ white

wings_____ to my im - mor - tal

home. ____ Oh, bear me a -

way on your snow ____ white wings _____ to

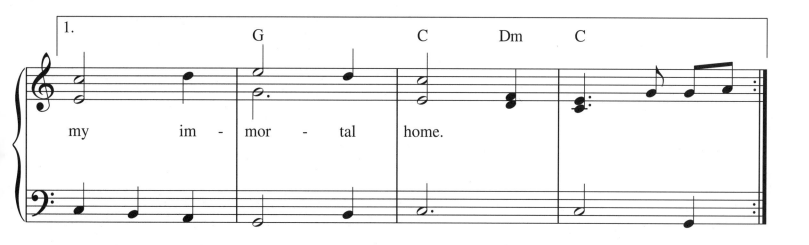

1.

my im - mor - tal home.

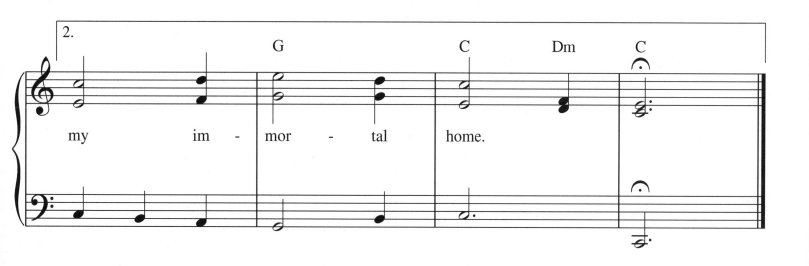

2.

my im - mor - tal home.